Understanding
i-KIDS

Understanding i-KIDS

DORIS SETTLES

PELICAN PUBLISHING COMPANY
GRETNA 2011

First published as *Virtual Parenting*, 2009
First Pelican edition, 2011

*The word "Pelican" and the depiction of a pelican
are trademarks of Pelican Publishing Company, Inc.,
and are registered in the U.S. Patent and Trademark Office.*

ISBN 978-1-58980-998-7

Printed in the United States of America
Published by Pelican Publishing Company, Inc.
1000 Burmaster Street, Gretna, Louisiana 70053

Dedication

Hubby, your belief that I can accomplish anything made this possible. Turns out, you are right!

Contents

1. Basic Skills...............................9

2. Barriers..................................25

3. It's Not Just About Access.....................41

4. The un-Geek's Guide to Technology........65

5. A Day in the Life of a Connected Teen....85

6. The Education Connection.....................93

7. Cyber-Safety.............................113

8. The Learning Spiral...........................135

Rules of Thumb.........................141

Online Resources.........................143

Glossary of Terms.........................147

CHAPTER ONE
Basic Skills

Parenting virtually isn't much different than just parenting; both keep us young and full of joy, usually.

Technology is great, but common sense is better! All of my life I've had a love affair with technology. I also love my family. But technology can do things for me they cannot—and vice versa—and technology can enhance my life with them and relationship to them, and others, like nothing else.

On the other hand, I can really hate technology. When it doesn't work it is an absolute nightmare. You know what I mean—you've been there too. Years ago a cartoon drawing circulated on email of a duck, hammer in hand, poised to smash a computer monitor. The caption said "Hit Enter." Everyone who has ever used a computer—for anything—knows how that duck is feeling at that very moment. But it doesn't stop us from coming back, again and again, because even though that level of frustration can drive us to do things we wouldn't ordinarily entertain, when the problem is resolved, we are back in love with the idea that our lives have been and continue to be enhanced.

The World Wide Web (the files, pages, software, etc. that we actually see when we log on) and the Internet (the physical hardware: servers, modems, wires, routers, etc. where the files live or transfer between) are really not such a technological barrier that our society cannot learn to manage and even control its impact. Is it moving us forward faster? I believe so. Can we keep up with the pace and maintain cultural mores and values? I hope so. Are we doing that now? Not so much.

First, let me join the chorus of technophiles and digital literacy researchers and everyone under age 18 to say exactly what you expect us to say: THE INTERNET IS HERE TO STAY. Trust me…it isn't going away. It will definitely change, expand, warp into something even more amazing, but the basic global connectivity it has brought us, barring a global electrical blackout, will not disappear. Not tomorrow. Not ever. And I, for one, am at once ecstatic and terrified to see the future it will bring. So should you be.

But what many frequently forget is that THE F2F WORLD IS NOT GOING AWAY EITHER! That proposal from the one person in the world you want to spend the rest of your life with, that final interview for the dream job—will likely happen in a F2F environment rather than online, although even in those areas there is movement in that direction. It is our job as parents to remind our children there is a F2F world, and to teach them where the "off" button is once in a while (not all the time), and to set the boundaries so that they have freedom to experiment in ways that minimize the risk of harm.

In my opinion, and in the opinion of most parenting and family researchers, good parenting with or without technology can be boiled down to three critical concepts, the first of which is:

Being There

Being there means creating and maintaining an open line of communication and dialogue with your children that actively engages them in the conversation, goal setting, decision-making and other things that are required as critical facets of the growing-up process. Put bluntly, they need our help and we can't help if we aren't there for them. If we don't know what's going on in their lives. If we don't appreciate their lows and highs as real and overwhelming and scary and wonderful and frustrating and amazing in the world that they live in. They do not live in an adult world as adults. Mostly, they're doing the best they can with what they have. But we as the adults could do so much more, if only we took the time.

Growing up is the most fundamental youth-adult partnership. It's been around a long time and isn't likely to stop happening anytime soon. But parents are busy people, confronted with what, in their minds, are real problems and issues that take precedence over worrying about the math test or basketball game or something someone might or might not have said about or to your child or a friend. The fact is…these are real problems and issues for your child. From an adult perspective they seem trivial and even amusing at times, but the things that concern your child are real nonetheless.

Alas, our youth has flown by, and we long for the perceived freedom and lack of responsibility our children have. Under major stress, many parents find themselves even envying their child what appears to us to be a stress-free life. But that is our perception, not theirs. Parents are blessed—and cursed—with having been able to experience life both from the carefree youth perspective, and from the ulcer-creating stress of the adult life.

Fundamentals of youth-adult partnerships require engaging youth, and engaging with youth to create something wonderful that benefits both. Youth-Adult partnerships can take several forms. All are appropriate given the situation and availability of resources. But all are very different in perspective of Being There.

Consider:
- Youth activities that have youth participating in a minor way. Adults think of the activity, plan the activity and implement the activity with or for youth. Can you think of any youth programs like this? There are many: school trips, summer camps, youth representatives on adult boards, etc.
- Youth activities that have adults supporting the activity with financing, transportation, logistics, etc.. These are thought of, planned and implemented by youth and have adults in a supporting role for the most part. This is also done widely

in school clubs, faith-based youth groups, and others.

- Youth or adult activities that use and value input from both adults and youth to think of, plan, and implement the event without tipping the balance toward one group or the other. These, for the most part, are rare.

Being there means being a passive and active participant in your child's world on a daily, weekly and monthly basis. It means participating in your child's world on the same levels you expect your child to participate in the family. You don't expect your five-year-old to support the family, but you certainly might expect him or her to put away things, prioritize responsibly, help pick movies for family film night, plan and participate in cooking meals or weekly shopping, as well as having input into family vacations or décor.

Conversely, your teenager doesn't expect you to do homework (I hope), take phone calls from friends, drop everything to chauffer him or her around, go to school dances or parties with friends (although I would never discourage you from attending, you won't and should not be there as a friend). However, your teen might appreciate help getting started on a writing assignment, selecting classes for next year, scheduling access to a family car or finances, and more. And he or she likely doesn't care about the trials and tribulations YOU had to face as a teenager who had to (and this is my father's voice here), "Carry my shoes around my neck to save on shoe leather, erase my papers every night to have clean paper the next day, get up at 4am to milk the cows, and walk in snowdrifts 4 feet deep 5 miles to school — uphill both ways — five days a week." Do you think we believed that? Not a chance. But it still makes me smile and rethink what tagline I want my children to remember me for!

There are many websites and resources that help you learn how to put in place the fundamentals of what in research circles is known as "Positive Youth Development" principles. These are listed in the Resources section of this book.

But to begin with, here are some ideas:

- Let your children know what some of the problems you are facing are, even asking and seriously listening, for their input and suggestions.

Take the perspective that these are family issues, not just yours. If expenses need to be trimmed, ask the children to participate in turning out lights, taking on extra duties, thank them for their participation and help with a special treat out of some of the savings.

- Text with your child if you've given them a cell phone, Nintendo DS or other communication device that uses texting. They don't email.

- Talk about technology and technology use. Engage them in helping you find technological answers to your daily tasks. Discuss new technologies and the many formats they take. Before allowing access to a particular game or website, ask your child to give you a tour and be present when he or she sets up the account.

- Take your son or daughter to dinner once a month. Just the two of you. Make it somewhere special for both you and your child. Discuss positive things—goals, dreams, current loves, travel—whatever keeps you both laughing.

- Schedule private time at home each day. Get up early and do a devotional together, religious or otherwise, and discuss concerns for the day and ways to approach them. My husband and our son always had a time at night where they caught up and shared ideas and issues. I used the car to have discussions both fun and serious. We were both captive audiences.

- Plan family F2F and online activities together that are fun for everyone, then follow through with participating gladly and with verve. Remember, I said fun for everyone!

Next in the basics for parenting well virtually, is the concept of: vlog? Do you have any idea what I just asked? Most any twelve-year-old wouldn't remember any of these, but would know exactly what I asked.

Being Aware

FACT: Kids are the digital natives, and everyone over 20 is a digital immigrant.

Think of it in these terms — do you remember the first email you sent? The first txt? Your first blog or vlog? Do you have any idea what I just asked?

We aren't aware of what our kids are doing in the virtual world because we just aren't native to it. It's as simple as that. Kids are naturally — and this isn't unique to this generation—early adopters. For a lot of reasons, they gravitate to and want to immerse themselves in whatever is new, bright, glitzy, cool, savvy, etc. And these days, that's technology. There is much more about this in Chapter 3.

But for now, let's just focus on the fact that adults for the most part don't use technology in the same way, and aren't as ready to accept the changes it requires, as youth are. I think we can agree on that. We love our technology, but we hate to upgrade. Digital natives have no such fears or constraints. Upgrading is the name of the game.

Every previous generation of parents since 1440 (see Chapter 2) has been able to say that they had once been six, twelve, fifteen—and make a case for understanding the world their kids live in. Not true today. That is not to say that we can't become socialized into this new way of thinking and reacting in time and space, but it won't be easy and we'll never be native.

These suggestions may help you become more aware:
- Understand that just being home with a computer doesn't mean children are safe.

- Spend some time each week reading technology culture blogs or listening to them on — dare I say it — an MP3 player.
- Surf the websites your kids go to regularly and see the kind of things — good and bad — that appear. Talk about what you saw — both good and bad — with your child (another method of Being There)
- Find some colleagues or friends that do things online that you do not, particularly fun things, and learn more about why and how.
- Do some searching around on videos and blog reading to see the wide variety of excellent programming as well as junk that really exists.

As the digital immigrants we need to recognize that, after all, this is and always will be an alien culture. But that doesn't mean we can't generate survival skills and indeed over time begin to feel comfortable in it, if not native. But it is very important to realize that technology is is no longer separate from the world we live in. Web 2.0 has moved us into a world that is no longer grounded (pun intended) in the F2F world. The online and the offline world is blended together with this always-on, always-connected, anytime, anywhere, everywhere, all the time and completely boundary-less virtual existence, and our physical life that is limited by time and space.

Giving access to the Internet without appropriate safeguards in place, which requires knowledge of what the dangers are, is the virtual equivalent of sending our eight and nine-year-olds to Europe...or China...or Africa...alone and unchaperoned. We don't know where our kids are and we haven't a clue how to protect and guide them in the vast expanse that is the Internet.

And that is our charge as parents, which leads us to the third and final basic skill of good parenting.

Being the Parent

You're the parent. You're footing the bill. And you are the one that is ultimately in control of and responsible for what and how your family uses technology. But you need ground under your feet to gain firm footing when you take a stance.

Whether they want to admit it or not, kids want us in their lives, both online and off. They do need our patient and responsible guidance and experience to help them make sense of the world. Researchers have been abundantly clear on that issue. But parenting isn't about being a best buddy or trying to recapture lost youth. It's about accepting responsibility for the life you have brought into the world and becoming the mentor, role model and monitor they need us to be.

Just as we watch out for our kids when we help them learn to cross the street in the physical world, we need to be watching what they are doing in the virtual world. And they need to know we are there…supporting them, guiding them, parenting them…physically and virtually.

Parenting virtually does mean:
- Monitoring activity online, just as we monitor what they do in the physical world.
- Working together with our children to set limits according to what they have proven they are capable of handling responsibly.
- Modeling appropriate behavior in the online world, such as creating your own profile on your child's favorite social networking site that follows clear safety parameters and insisting that any-

one you link to follows those same rules.

- Helping keep the online world safe by reporting abuse, which is easy and efficient, while not totally effective, on every social networking website.
- Placing the computer in a highly visible area of your home, such as your family room or kitchen, and limiting use in private areas.
- Collecting and turning off cell phones at a certain time each night. One friend has a long power strip on the kitchen counter where all cell phones must go when her family comes home, turned off and waiting for the next day. She has 11 children in her home!

Kids see the abundant benefit in the new Web 2.0 culture. But typical to all younger generations…they dismiss or minimize the very real dangers and problems that technology brings with it. That's our job as parents — to look out for them and to teach them that the world isn't all marshmallows and candy canes. And frequently, as adults have since Aristotle's day, we overreact and want to change things back to the way they were…to OUR way. In this context, it means removing access…pulling the plug.

I will never advocate pulling the plug. I am a firm believer that technology has and does and will bring better things to how we work and live, and by preventing access to it for our kids we short-circuit their ability to learn to live wisely and safely in an ever-increasingly technological world. Shutting our eyes to the potential benefits that might be gained only exacerbates the problem.

Technology doesn't have to be the problem; technology just might be the answer.

CHAPTER 2
Barriers

Lack of understanding is a barrier, waiting to be overcome.

So why is there this digital generation gap? What are the barriers for us as parents that prevent us from understanding and participating in the cultures our kids are embracing more each day? What are the unique perceptions and qualities of youth that make them drive us so totally crazy?

The purpose of this entire book is to detail and hopefully help you understand those concepts and barriers that give context to the virtual culture and its relationship to today's *digital natives* (those under 20) and the *digital immigrants* (the rest of us). Each chapter in some way provides insight into barriers, and each chapter is written in the hope that you will gain perspective into those concepts in order to provide you with a foundation for parenting in this new, blended virtual/physical world in which we now live.

The most obvious barrier is that the media, researchers and sales departments have created a double-dilemma for adults who work with youth today, over-whelming you with facts for which there is very little if any context and striking fear into your hearts (a con-demned-if-you-do, condemned-if-you-don't situation) rather than providing information to help you make educated and responsible decisions concerning technol-ogy in your homes and lives.

These are the two camps that guide and direct most of our knowledge base and emotional relationship with technology. Both have merit and each is right about technology, but each is too simplistic in its view. In or-der to make good decisions, we need a context for and from both camps into which this information. Increas-ingly, though, context-starved parents take one of two roads: either pulling the plug or turning their heads. Neither is an appropriate response for today's parent, whose job it is to guide and mentor children into re-sponsible adulthood. Today, like it or not, technology is a part of that journey.

- *More is Better Camp:* There are those who be-lieve the ubiquitous use of technology as the great equalizer, and the lack of it driving further wedges between the *Haves* and the *Have-Nots*. And they're right…it can and does both. Instructional technology and distance learning research has shown us that students who would not normally take part in a F2F class discussion are much more willing to participate in an online discussion. In social networking sites and IM protocols, we see kids trying out multiple identities to see which fits the typical adolescent persona-of-the-day method of "finding themselves" in ways they could never do in the F2F world. However, for those denied technology access, when it comes time for students to move into higher education, work or business settings, they are increasingly unable to be successful without technology remediation.

But as I detail in the next chapter, it's not just about providing access. It's about understanding how this tool is changing the practices of our daily lives and therefore impacting our culture…and being involved in a real and personal way, as parents, to guide and teach our kids what safe and responsible behavior looks like whenever and wherever they have access. And it's about the intricacies and opportunities that access provides and how it might impact each of us personally, affect our messages, expand our relationships (in good and bad ways), coping with the hardware and networking issues that are unavoidable, and finding a balance for the always-on, always-connected culture we have been thrust into. It's about deciding who is in control — the technology or us?

- *It's All Bad Camp* — Everywhere you look there is a new show or article or awareness effort to demonstrate how easy it is for child pornographers, predators, identity thieves or other miscreants to wipe out your life savings, or rape, sodomize and murder your five-year-old. The idea seems to be that scaring people to death will somehow make them take the Internet more seriously. It's working. The idea that your ten-year-old might accidentally run across serious Internet porn turns the stomachs of most parents. And it should. Even scarier is that our teenagers are creating it themselves and posting it online themselves. But pulling the plug does not make it go away. Previous technologies that were media-rich (TV, Movies, Radio, Newspapers) had content filters in place before troublesome content reached the viewer. Cable TV...long touted as easy pornography access to children...found a way to separate and secure those channels so four-year-olds across the nation won't end up watching Bill and Monica in anime as they surf channels on Saturday mornings watching cartoons.

The Internet, as it becomes increasingly user-created content, has no such filters, and the debate rages on about whether there should be...indeed, whether there *can* be. There are ways to block sites, but they are largely ineffective over time as kids and hackers figure out workarounds. I'm always amused when I do a training to educators and someone smugly says, "We don't have a MySpace problem...it's blocked at our school." She (or he) is stunned when other participants regale her with stories of hacking, proxies, off-campus access such as public libraries and friends' houses, and more.

Before I delve into the bricks and mortar (pun intended) that built and hold fast these barriers in place, here is a quick sampling of some of the reasons why we digital immigrants and digital natives are having a hard time communicating what is really a completely divergent worldview.

1. **Give a child a hammer and everything's a nail—** The Web is changing how we work and socialize and communicate and more. Weaving historical perspective with modern-day realities, compare how adults and youth bring different mindsets to the benefits (and drawbacks) of progress in any age, and therefore different pluses and minuses. For youth, technology is a hammer just looking for a way to apply it—and the nail is their life. This is probably the biggest barrier to guiding our youth toward successfully and responsibly adapting to the virtual environment. Some concepts transfer easily and well from the physical to the virtual environment. Some just don't. As adults, we really do have to learn to adapt to the world our children not only understand, but are already hammering away on!

2. **The Sky is Falling!** — As far back as Aristotle adults have issued dire warnings about the future of the world if put in the hands of the current generation of youth. Guess what...we've survived. But until the last two decades or so, there have been many adults in the worlds of youth to befriend and mentor them safely to adulthood. Today, technology has created a world where youth are left completely to their own devices...and they know it! It's called online social networking, massive multiplayer gaming, virtual realities, and more. A place where online bullying, pornography created and posted by teens, a glut of personal information useful to scumbags anywhere, and a dearth of F2F relationships are the norm for today's youth. Adults don't inhabit those places — not because they aren't worth inhabiting but because they aren't comfortable there — and so the kids are on their own.

3. **Technology doesn't always mean being a geek** — I am always amazed when people refer to me as a technology guru. I promise you I am no such thing, whatever that might be. I have a colleague and friend that, when we're together,

always introduces me with a new geeky descriptor: "This is Doris, the Computer Queen" or "I'd like to introduce you to Doris, the MySpace Diva." Perhaps I use more technology and know more about technological innovation and culture than most people might, but I am not embarrassed to admit that I can't even get my home network printer to print from my laptop. In fact, when this problem first started, I called my son...then in the middle of a Ph.D. in Artificial Intelligence, and asked him how to fix the problem. His answer? "Mom...I've told you over and over...I am not a networking person. Different fields altogether. I can't get my laptop to print from our network either!" The goal is to separate out technology areas and expertise, breaking the overwhelming volume that hits parents into manageable bits, demystifying some of the concepts, jargon, fields and requirements. Letting go of the things you don't really need to know enables you to focus on what's really important.

4. **The more things change, the more they stay the same** — Good parenting or successful living really hasn't changed. What has changed is that

we are all-to-ready to use technology to replace good parenting and a full life. I recently sat beside a young couple at a restaurant in the Atlanta airport who had a 9-month old lovely little boy. But instead of engaging their son in the activities going on around them and with and between them, they opened up a DVD player and hit play...and Barney's massive purple body took the boy away from everyone and everything around him. Yes, the parents might have been able to eat more peacefully, but what did the child learn? Barney was telling him how to behave and get along with other people, but the parents whose job it was to put Barney's words into context in the real and physical world had abandoned him.

5. **The Always-ON Connection** — online social networking (the MySpace phenomenon) has grown to epic proportions with the world, especially youth. I talk to kids and parents at school assemblies and conferences all over and am always struck at how few adults inhabit the social networking sites. We allowed our kids to go to malls to "hang out" because we knew there were physical safety nets if there was a problem...sales

people, mall security, etc. Little of that exists online — it's a free-for-all, and it isn't entirely the fault of the technology providers. Created for artists and musicians, MySpace was stunned when it was wholesale adopted by youth — the obvious audience for musicians. Yes, technology will continue to refine and develop new ways of making our online experiences more secure and more safe, but those among us whose minds are always looking for ways to do harm are also re-fining and developing new ways around those roadblocks.. And it's high time we create an adult presence to be able to take advantage of those "teachable moments" which always come with parental involvement in our children's lives.

6. **Say Whaaaat??** — Technospeak is the language of computers, but that language has many dialects and it is evolving every moment of every day. Networking people deal with P2Ps, WAPs, USBs, servers and more. If you want to buy a new com-puter you need to know how much RAM, VRAM, and DRAM you want, not to mention whether you've decided on a trackball or Opti-cal mouse. Log onto the Internet, and you need to use a browser that will find a secure URL for

you to buy that new GPS device, after you've googled the reviews and scanned the hits. Programmers use VBasic, PHP, ASP, Perl, and other similarly obtuse acronyms. And looking over little Cindy's shoulder as she IMs with her best friend Erin, you read her conversation:

> C: How R U?
>
> E: IDK
>
> C: LOL. U nvr no
>
> E: GMAB
>
> C: P911. TTYL

And wonder what that was all about. A recent Pew Trust study showed that over 70% of Americans still did not know the term "phishing," one of the most insidious of Internet scams.

7. **Finding balance in a world that never sleeps** — I recently attended a conference where the founder of 25 Lanterns, a nonprofit association that provides solar lanterns to women of Afghanistan to improve their lives, spoke about her experiences as a photojournalist there and how she saw the need for the organization. It seems

she was assigned to a very remote area of Afghanistan, where there was no electricity, no running water, no kerosene lanterns, no access to any kind of modern convenience or technology. When the sun went down at 6:00pm…you went to sleep because you could not see to do anything else. Her comment was that it was the most unproductive time of her life, and was overwhelmingly frustrating. Most of us today, being catapulted back to pioneer days, would chafe pretty quickly. But most of us also need how to turn our stressful, technology-glutted lives OFF so we can rest and refresh. Our kids don't. They really don't know how. This is their society in a way we won't ever truly understand…because having an OFF time has been part of our experience in a way it has never been part of theirs. But research is clear that we need that OFF time, so it is incumbent upon us to help our kids understand the need for it and find a way to merge ON with OFF in a way that makes sense to this new culture…and not just because we said *"TURN IT OFF!"*

The Luddite View

Adults, for better or for worse, tend to become more rigid and less spontaneous or innovative as they age. We like change in moderation; we fear rapid or systemic change. Today's term Luddite stems from the 19th century English textile craftsmen who rioted in the vicinity of Nottingham, England beginning in 1811 to destroy the labor-saving textile machinery that they feared was replacing them. Today, the term applies to anyone who fears technology or technology changes.

During the Industrial Revolution, itself a technological restructuring, people feared the change for real and basic survival reasons.

1. They feared being replaced in their jobs by machinery.
2. They feared the loss of quality in products.
3. They feared a marked increase in price of products.
4. They feared the de-humanization of the workplace.

In retrospect, were any of these fears well-grounded? Well, there has been a decrease in product quality perhaps, but pricing has fallen to the point where products are less expensive to replace than repair. Jobs have changed, but there is no less need for humans in the workforce — someone has to make the machines and someone has to tell them what to do. And as for the de-humanization of the workplace, those humans have to be there somewhere — they just don't answer the phones any more — the machines are doing that and we humans are consigned to wander in the matrix they create for us. When was the last time you actually got a human being the first time you called your utilities company or your bank?

Luddites have been with us ever since, and some of them make very valid points. Tipper Gore advocated for greater censorship in radio and television. Charlie Chaplin's film *Modern Times* is a classic reflection on technological progress. *Silent Spring* by Rachel Carson became an altar call for the green movement. And in the 1950's, the Federal Teachers organization said:

> "*Ballpoint pens will be the ruin of education in our country. Students use these devices and then throw them away. The American values of thrift and frugality are being disregarded. Businesses and banks will never allow such expensive luxuries.*"

And one more barrier that is entirely human. Even when we try to work with anyone else (not just our children) on a computer, the temptation to wrest away the mouse and take control is very nearly overwhelming. Remember the TV commercial with the little girl who takes the mixing spoon away from Mom and says, "Mother, I can do it myself"? But by taking control of the mouse, you take control of the learning experience, and short-circuit the possibility for your child to learn (or whomever you're trying to work with at the time). Remember that the next time your hand starts moving toward somebody else's mouse.

I hope these starting points are beginning dispel the fear and bring down the barriers that are preventing you from engaging in the virtual environment with your kids. Focus on those technology areas that are comfortable to you. Learn a new skill that will help you to do your work or personal interactions.

Just stop trying to ignore it altogether and hoping it will go away. It won't.

CHAPTER THREE
It's Not Just About Access

If the medium is the message, then what are we saying?

I don't think I can emphasize this often enough. Access is a given. The overwhelming acceptance of web-enabled cell phone technology provides anytime/anywhere portability of a virtual life. If you don't provide Internet access at home, you can bet there is a friend's house where your child can log on. Or they can go to the Public Library. And then there's the probability that there is high-speed access at school and many ways around the blocks and safeguards designed and purported to limit access to inappropriate sites.

In addition, the expansion of mass media from the days of Gutenberg to the present has created not only increasing access to information and each other, but an increase in awareness beyond our local communities and growing global social responsibility. We know more about what is going on outside our own physical boundaries, and if we wish, we can make a difference in the lives of people we've never met and never will meet. Indeed, this is a "brave new world."

However, many times, content providers (the people who create websites) do not spend enough time analyzing and considering how the medium changes the interaction between audience and information, and either simply make an effort to replicate the printed medium through PDFs and documents, losing out on the opportunity to expand the interactivity of links, multimedia and alternative formats that the Web provides, or go whole hog overboard...creating visual overload from which the user cannot begin to separate out the specific information they might have come to find.

The advent of Web 2.0 — user created content — makes anyone a content provider. No special equipment, no special knowledge, no special software, no special permission is required to post musings from anyone and everyone worldwide — without credentials, without research, and sometimes without a whole lot of common sense.

I mean, who really wants to read all that teen angst? Ask a teenager why and they'll likely respond "I have nothing to hide." I've asked that very question of dozens of teens, and more often than not, that's the answer. But why do they feel the need to document every waking moment and every incidental thought process and every heart-rending emotion for the world? Got me. Most writers are avid journalers. Not me. I tried keeping a diary once and my sister found it. Then I tried journaling as a mother and my stepson found it. Neither time was pretty, so there is no way I am going to go there. But kids love it. They can, so they do. And its our job to help them understand that just because they can doesn't mean they should.

A colleague, after attending a workshop I'd given, went online to her daughter's social networking profile. Keep in mind her daughter is 23 years old. She was astonished at how much personal information her daughter was putting out there for anyone to run across…and for her regular visitors to peruse. She addressed the "What've I got to hide?" response with going to her daughter's favorite celebrity's website and really analyzing the personal information shared there. In reality, there wasn't much. Fans did not really know his thoughts, emotions, daily activities, etc. Her point that if someone who made his living off people knowing about him wasn't sharing, then neither should her daughter. Smart mom!

We are application-oriented and technology is just chock full of application. But while we might be looking at the same technologies, do we see the same applications and benefits as our youth? And do we see the risks and barriers that using those technologies might present to us as individuals as well as a society? Probably not.

The Digital Generation Gap

There is a very real and present Digital Divide. In fact, I believe there are two. But for the purposes of this book I am not focusing on the one usually talked about in the worlds of economic and education research that sees technology access as the great equalizer, and the lack of it driving wedges between the *haves* and the *have-nots*. They are right, technology can and does both. There is that facet of a digital divide.

But there is another digital divide that is more philosophic and cultural than economic: the Digital Generation Gap. True, keeping up with technology takes money and access to technology makes one more viable and connected to a global economy. But the advent of an always-on environment has created a break between generations in ways similar to previous generations, but different in some critical and fairly obscure ways.

Adults and youth have always seen things differently.

> *"I see no hope for the future of our people if they are dependent on frivolous youth of today, for certainly all youth are reckless beyond words... When I was young, we were taught to be discreet and respectful of elders, but the present youth are exceedingly wise [disrespectful] and impatient of restraint"* (Hesiod, 8th century BC).

My own adolescence was marked with the advent of the Beatles, long hair, LSD, free love, communes and ever more abhorrent practices that had my parents terrified and aghast all at once. Like Hesiod, Aristotle, Socrates, Ben Franklin and more throughout history, each new generation of parents is faced with new challenges in how we think and perceive the world through the lens of our experience versus the ebullience of youth.

But the world has changed in one very significant way with the advent of Web 2.0 technology in a way it has not changed since 1440 when Gutenberg invented the printing press. Let me explain this in an analogy to the F2F world.

Web 1.0 is like a library. When you go into the library, you are looking for information to take away with you not physically but mentally. You read a book, put it back, and leave. The library has not changed in any significant way. Nothing has been added, removed or modified. The only one who can do that is the librarian. You are changed by the addition of knowledge.

In Web 2.0, however, the library is easily added to, removed from, and modified by anyone anywhere anytime. In effect, we have all become librarians.

Adults view technology as a tool, still existing in a Web 1.0 world where technology is primarily a resource. This is a natural outcome of the industrial revolution when technology was seen as a means to make work more efficient. The luddite's fear that technology will replace humans has been overcome, but the mindset that technology's purpose is to provide tools with which to make our work easier and more effective remains.

We search for answers to questions. We use online information to help us make a decision about what to buy (but we may still go to the local bricks-and-mortar store to purchase it). We use email to set up meetings, cell phones to tell others when we're running late, or catch up on the news online. Notwithstanding a recent study that found that cell phones actually may not be keeping us on time and efficient at work and play, we relish the ease and proficiency that technology tools offer to facilitate what we do to look and feel more productive and more professional.

Today's youth also see that benefit. But, typical to seeing everything as a nail for their technological hammer, they have taken it a step further to integrate technology not just into how they can work smarter, faster, bigger, easier but into how they build and maintain relationships with each other and the world. In other words, technology no longer just improves *how* they live, it *is how they live together.*

This difference is huge, and far-reaching for today and tomorrow.

And no wonder. The generations born before

1981 grew up in a world that, even with television, radio and the telephone linking us together, existed almost exclusively in the physical realm. Those born in 1988 and beyond have always had the opportunity to easily, inexpensively talk to anyone anywhere anytime, linking them to an electronic world that is completely separate from their physical one — and yet simultaneous to it. They meet new friends, interact, exchange pictures, music, interests in a similar way to physical interaction, but they may never actually physically share the same space.

A simple Venn diagram demonstrates how adults and youth use technology in different ways and how their technology use overlaps.

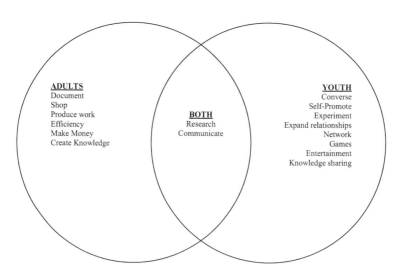

Email is an excellent illustration of how adults and youth can both be very technologically savvy in very different ways.

To most of the adult community, *"You've Got Mail"* means we've got email in our inbox. Just about everybody's got email today. It's how we are productive and how we document what gets done, when, how and by whom in much of the business community. Adults holster their Treos, Iphones and Blackberries to be sure we don't miss an email and so we can respond instantly. For the most part, the adult business world revolves around email.

As a rule, youth don't use email. And as social networking increases, they are using it less and less. An 8th grade girl told me recently that she only used her email account for two things: to sign up for things and to communicate with adults. She rarely checks it. The other students around her agreed.

Just this morning I had a call from a colleague looking for the email address of a youth to help her in a training event she was facilitating next week. I called a friend to ask if her son would be interested, and she told me to message him through his online social networking profile. He has an email account — several in fact — but checks them rarely if ever. Both my colleague and I have profiles on that social network, so I messaged them both to get in touch with each other. Problem solved. But if we had relied on email, we never would have gotten through to each other.

This shift from email to video messaging or text messaging is one that adults, for the most part, haven't made. There are good reasons for that lack of interest.

- Messaging is real-time so it requires us to drop what we're doing and respond...or be present online to "talk" rather than reading/responding when convenient
- Messaging is a quick and rapid-fire conversation, so it requires more effort
- Messaging doesn't provide the same level of physical documentation email does
- Messaging is faster and less thoughtful so also more easily misunderstood

- Messaging is less formal and therefore less businesslike

Youth and adults are using technology in different ways because they have grown up with technology meaning different things in their lives. That isn't going to change—today's youth will use technology differently as adults than their children will as new technologies surface for them to co-opt into their own culture and lifestyle. But that's how we adapt. But we need to understand the distinctions between this "new" world and the "old" one to be able to be effective parents.

This concept is critical to both the *Being There* and *Being Aware* effective parenting strategies. Without an understanding of the differences between the way youth and adults perceive and use technology, we cannot effectively communicate with them about responsible and safe use of that technology.

The virtual world has no physical boundaries. Our kids are sitting in their bedrooms talking to people all over the world. They may be accessing information we would never allow them access to in our physical worlds. All while we, as parents, are glad they are "safe" at home.

Environmental Differences

The physical and virtual worlds, while in many ways similar, are in many respects diametrically opposed. The safety skills we teach our children in the physical world do not automatically transfer into the virtual one. And so we need to consider what new skills today's youth might need in order to stay safe and be responsible as virtual citizens.

These distinctions have both positive and negative aspects. And as adults we need to see both sides so we can respond accordingly.

Let's take them one at a time.

Unchaperoned:

Youth know that this social milieu is largely uninhabited by their parents or other adults who know and care about them. So their fear of misbehaving is all but eliminated. Not that I advocate fear as a behavior modification tool — but any anthropologist or social scientist will tell you that cultures are built on social norms, and those norms continue to exist as long as the ramifications for acting outside those social norms are more harmful than the benefit of those actions: fear of consequences.

Benefits: Youth see this as a huge benefit. They can do what they want, when they want without adult interference. They can try out different personas and push the envelope without that "fear" of social consequences. It's an adolescent dream-come-true.

Drawbacks: Obviously, we cannot hope to keep the virtual environment safe for our kids if we aren't even there. It is the equivalent in the physical world of sending today's youth unchaperoned on trips to New York City, Bangkok, Tel Aviv, Acapulco and more. When I do trainings at mixed-age audiences, I ask everyone to stand up, then tell everyone that has a MySpace or

Facebook page to sit down. Guess who's left standing. Right—the adults.

Being There, Being Aware Actions: Adults need to be modeling and monitoring responsible behavior in the online environment, just as we do in the physical environment. Every time I get on a social networking site, I find profiles by adults that have inappropriate content. If every adult spent half an hour a month perusing social networking sites for inappropriate content, underage users, etc. these would be safer environments for our youth to inhabit. Create your own profiles in online social environments, then search, click and become completely familiar with how it works and its content. What you see will inform and provide conversation between you and your children.

Anonymity:

The Internet strips us of our five senses that provide confirmation that information we are receiving in the physical world is true and accurate. From the perceived safety of our homes or classrooms, we can interact with others in ways we would never consider acting in the physical environment, even if we were afforded the opportunity. This, as you can imagine, has both benefits and drawbacks.

Benefits: Distance learning research has demonstrated for over two decades that students who would not normally take part in a classroom discussion feel freer to participate in online discussions behind the protection of their computer screens. In social networking sites and IM profiles, we see kids creating multiple profiles to try out different personalities in order to better define who they are and what they believe. Youth of the '70s tried to "find themselves" by dressing, talking and behaving differently than their peers or parents from day to day. Today's youth have the opportunity to try out these differences in persona simultaneously and in variations and combinations that are absolutely unlimited.

Drawbacks: The obvious detriment here is that we

no longer have use of our five senses to help warn us when we are nearing danger. The girlfriend your daughter is talking to online may, in fact, be 65 and a sexual predator. In addition, the mass media has pushed the envelope of behavior beyond what is socially acceptable and so cyber-bullying or inappropriate behavior are commonplace.

Being There, Being Aware Actions: Talk with your children about how the computer provides a smoke screen for people who want to use the Internet for illegal or immoral activity. Just as students are tweaking their "truths" as they move about online, others are doing the same. Look at the information they are posting and discuss how someone might use it against them, whether that person is someone they know in the F2F world or someone they do not.

Digital Citizenship:

For the most part, printed material offers to its readers pre-analyzed, pre-synthesized and pre-contextualized content to digest, censored for content and suitability. The Internet moves us beyond printed material to a smorgasbord of resources that is completely uncensored.

Benefits: Without the intervention of censorship and geographic restrictions, we have wider access to a much larger and broader range of materials than mankind has ever been able to draw from.

Drawbacks: This morass of information, despite the best efforts of natural language processing researchers, remains to a large extent un-contextualized, un-analyzed and un-synthesized. We must be better able to analyze and contextualize ourselves or be drowned in the ocean of too much information, or potentially too much mis-information. Critical thinking skills are ever more important in the smorgasbord of offerings presented to us online.

Being There, Being Aware Actions: As parents, we need to become aware of what is out there both to link our families to wonderful resources, knowledge and information previously unavailable and to protect our families from those who would invade our privacy and bring them harm. The only way to become aware is to be there — getting to know the online environment as well as we know our physical one. Setting rules about what technology is in our homes and how our families are to use those technologies help move us into developing the critical thinking skills and responsible behavior necessary to live well in the virtual world. Talk as a family about how to blend the physical and online environments in ways that enhance responsible citizenship for everybody.

Democratizing Authority:

And in the online world we are not just readers and writers but participants in a very real and tangible way...clicking our way through links to either get lost in the quagmire of possibilities or get to where we wanted to go. We can upload video taken with our cell phone cameras or comment on a friend's social networking profile or vent through our latest blog entry or add our two cents worth to a Wikipedia entry we think needs clarification. Authority is being democratized by allowing input from anyone and everyone worldwide — without credentials, without research, and without anyone's consent.

Benefits: America was founded on the principles of human rights. The Internet is validating and implementing those principles in ways we have never been able to do in the physical world. By its very nature, the Internet is altruistic. It provides a forum to share information, resources and develop relationships that can be, and often are, beneficial to all. If you ask me a question I cannot answer, but run across the answer online a month or so later, I can fire off an email to you with a link and make you happy. We can develop relationships with people living in far different cultures or time zones and promote our understanding and the understanding of others in ways that may help reduce strife and prejudice.

Drawbacks: Like Pandora's Box, the Internet opens the door to those who would spew forth the worst of human nature with pornography, hate sites, suicide, anorexia and bulimia support groups (I mean the ones that are encouraging, not discouraging these behaviors) and who would prey upon others.

Being There, Being Aware Actions: Just as Hope remained in Pandora's Box as a gift to mitigate the evils visited on the world when Pandora lifted the lid, increased presence of responsible adults in the online world provides the input needed to create communities that are safe and fun. Just because we *can* post something doesn't mean we *should* post it. The Internet doesn't exist in a vacuum—it is created, enhanced and inhabited by human beings. And as human beings, we have both a physical and virtual presence that is increasingly becoming one. As parents, merging those two worlds means considering parallels from the physical world we are comfortable with and how we generate guidelines and advice for our children in that environment, then applying those parallels to the virtual world to help them recognize the similarities and the differences. Helping our kids make informed, educated decisions has a ripple-effect in both their physical and virtual communities that can only benefit everyone.

Media issues:

Aside from the content overload, the technology itself can get in the way. Lack of technology literacy creates a two-edged sword: frustrated users expect what they find online to mirror what they see in print, and do not know how to control and manipulate the many options (links, multi-media, formats) in order to find and use what they want.

Being able to read and write opened the doors to knowledge in ways that could transform lives. Literacy no longer only means being able to read and write. Today it also means being able to navigate the Internet to locate that same knowledge, and much, much more. It means being able to be the content editor for what in the physical world would be too much information for a single library.

The online world is far more personal, portable and pervasive than the physical one in ways we are just beginning to understand. The limits we can place on our physical existence (a closed door, property lines, legal limitations) do not translate well into the virtual existence, where life never sleeps.

> *Benefits:* As developers and programmers become more literate about the ways in which technology impacts our perception of the message, better technology will be available to make content more user-friendly and accessible. And as users become more familiar with technology, we will be better able to process and synthesize information.

> *Drawbacks*: Technology today is having difficulty playing catch-up with the volume of use and op-

portunities it has already made available. And innocent web searches can turn up really scary websites that adults shouldn't see — not to mention kids. This country was founded with primarily a reactive legal system, one in which something needs to happen before it is addressed. Much discussion remains to take place about who should control the Internet, or even if it is controllable at any level. As the virtual world grows and new technologies emerge, these discussions will continue to evolve.

Being There, Being Aware Actions: Parents need to become the content editors that are missing on the Internet. Teaching responsible behavior means providing access to new behaviors slowly and as children are able to handle them. When your son or daughter turns 16 you don't just expect them to know how to drive and hand over the keys. There is a process by which new drivers are taught the rules of the road, given the opportunity to practice under supervision, and slowly allowed to develop as responsible drivers. Establishing rules, supervising online activity, being knowledgeable in their online activity and the activity of their friends allows you the opportunity to direct and guide their growth in their virtual life.

The reality is that your children *do* have access to the online environment, and they love it. Access is only going to be more available and more portable as technology improves.

Youth are, to their credit, finding ways to integrate online social networking into their physical environments that enhance and enlarge their personal potential. Educational possibilities are unlimited, and all of us now have the opportunity to truly experience a world without being limited by chronological, geographic or cultural boundaries. Understanding these opportunities is critical to effectively parenting with the basic concepts of *Being There, Being Aware and Being the Parent.*

We, too, have those same opportunities.

CHAPTER FOUR
The un-Geek's Guide to Technology

Geek 2.0: Savvy, sophisticated, dressed down because they need us more than we need them, navigating the world with technology. Gotta love 'em.

My first advice to you is to take a deep breath and release the belief that in order to use a new technology (or new to you) you have to know everything about how it works. You don't. You couldn't if you wanted to, and I cannot imagine why you would want to anyway. And more...you probably won't break it if you try it without understanding it. I have decided that this, like most belief systems, is a learned behavior. In my years of observing kids and computers, I have never met a fourth grader who said, when asked to do something with a computer he'd never tried before, "But what if I break it?" How many fifty- or sixty-somethings have said that very thing? Kids are naturally early adopters of anything new. Perhaps because they can't read the instruction manual (many times written by English-as-

Second-Language folks), it never crosses their minds to pore over the steps to make something happen. They just jump in there and do it.

And so do I...much to the chagrin of my parents and teachers. For example, when our parents gave my sisters and me identical video cameras in 1987 (huge things that nearly required a crane to get out of the box), my detail-oriented brother-in-law sat down and read the manual cover to cover. I, on the other hand, pulled out the camera, plugged it in, popped in a tape and started shooting...beginning with my brother-in-law reading the manual. When he had digested the directions two hours later and was ready to try out his new camera, it was defective. In my opinion, he wasted two hours! Two days later, with a new camera in hand, he just started filming with great zeal.

Fortunately, that's the perspective that most adults have: technology provides real and tangible benefit to us and to our children. But we need to seriously contemplate buying new technology with the same informed decision-making process we use to buy a new dishwasher or TV, where to go on our next vacation, or that new GPS system.

I was, and am, that *early adopter* who is always searching for what's coming down the pipeline for tomorrow — today. I probably come by that naturally. We are blessed to have family movies from the 1920s that my grandmother took with her brand-spanking-new video-8 camera. She wasn't the best videographer in the world (watching her footage of the Smokey Mountains taken during annual vacations gives me motion sickness), but she was relentless in capturing moments both large and small. We see my mother twirling her baton as she practiced for the band, my uncles raking leaves into a pile and burning them in the back yard, the family picnic in rural Morgan County, Kentucky as well as the New York Worlds Fair and trips to the Gulf of Mexico.

My father also contributed to my technologically-enhanced genetic pool. Among other things, we were the first in our neighborhood to have a color TV. It arrived on Halloween, and we invited the neighborhood in that evening to watch *Bonanza*, turning Hoss and Adam and Little Joe first green, then purple with great delight as my sugar high raged.

And while technology can be great fun and wildly entertaining, as I discovered on that Halloween night so very long ago, I don't recommend just running out and buying the latest, trendiest thing. I do have both a desktop and a laptop, various presentation hardware, a PDA that is my phone, camera, organizer and calendar, and have recently become the proud owner of a GPS.

All this comes at a cost—but I don't just mean the financial one. I spend a lot of time researching, evaluating and testing new technologies against a rigorous standard of "What's in it for me" until I am satisfied that I've gotten the best fit for my lifestyle and needs. But most important, it is technology I am certain will make a positive difference in the way I work, learn and live and that is truly beneficial for today and tomorrow.

What kind of equipment you need is directly associated with what you want to do with it…not what it can or might be able to do. You know that computer equipment is already outdated when it hits the store shelves, so trying to keep up with technology is already a losing proposition. Years ago, a friend told me she would buy a computer for her family when she didn't need to upgrade every year. Her philosophy had two holes in it. First, technology will always be improving so upgrades will always be necessary. Second, and most important for our purposes here, just because an upgrade exists doesn't mean you need it. Evaluating your family's needs for today and the near future (maybe two years out) and then building the technological environment around your needs is the correct approach.

Let's take another example from the physical world. You have only so much income that you can devote to housing. You've had all the children you expect to have, so your family size is set. But you realize that the house you are living in is cramped and making it impossible to enjoy each other. You have two girls and they've had it with sharing a room. As they get older and each acquires more "stuff" you envision the potential for overload. Your son has his own room, which is a major bone of contention with his sisters and causing family fights on a regular basis. Your kitchen is small and can only accommodate one person working at a time. As your kids grow into teens, you know they will become pickier eaters (and your son is already becoming a snackaholic — seeming to eat all day long) and require their own space to fix food. The family room is overflowing with seating for five, the big screen TV and a computer workstation taking up most of the floor space. There are constant fights about programming and access.

The handwriting is on the wall. You need to look for a new house with a different layout that will better suit your family's needs.

Now let's apply that same situation to technology. You have an Apple Classic (circa 1983) with a dot matrix printer and an ancient scanner. You are connected to the Internet through a telephone dialup connection. All you do on the computer is create a family newsletter which you snailmail to family and friends, so you are just fine with what you have, and obviously have been for a long, long time. You check email, get online and do other things through your work access. The kids, however, are spending a lot of time at friend's houses creating social networking profiles, chatting online with their friends, downloading ringtones for their cell phones and uploading video files. They'd love to stay home more, and some of their friend's mothers wouldn't mind a little peace and quiet. The kids are clamoring for high speed access and a more powerful system. They are embarrassed to take their papers to school printed on dot matrix. Can you blame them? Would you turn in a dot matrix proposal to your boss?

So, you go to your local mega-market for technology and begin to look at the options. Most of us think this is the next logical step. But it isn't. Becoming educated about options actually muddles the picture by creating information overload. The first step is to determine your needs, then match the technology to your lifestyle, not the other way around. Know exactly what you want to do with your technology before you walk into the store.

When you look at a house, you have the opportunity to picture yourself and your family living in the space. That's much more difficult when looking at technology. Like with a house, you don't want to move every few years to keep up with your needs. Well, I have one friend who moves every two years to be able to purge and thoroughly clean. Most of us are happy to live with the hidden dust bunnies. But with technology we don't really know what our needs are now, nor what they may be with the advent of new technologies down the road. This presents a dilemma which is more easily addressed than it appears at first glance.

Sit down with your family and ask questions to determine what your real needs are. Make sure you distinguish between "needs" and "wants" for this first pass. Each time your children, your wife, your husband become frustrated with his or her technology availability and access, consider these questions:

- Functional needs – What can or cannot be done with your current technology structure? What necessary functions aren't being provided by your current system? Is there a way to meet these needs through means other than a full-scale upgrade? Are there resources available elsewhere that can meet these needs temporarily or long-term?

- Technology needs - What is the availability of service support for your current and proposed technology upgrade? How much infrastructure do you have in place to address technology problems? How easily will the upgrade take place and how much of a learning curve will it require? How widely will it affect other users? Other technology? Other infrastructure such as electrical, space requirements, etc.

- Financial needs – What are your financial resources that can be devoted to technology? Remember to include support and extras such as software. Create a technology budget that is reasonable and works within the overall family budget.

But, you say, I can't even talk to those people once I do know what I need. Technospeak (my term) is indeed the language of the technologically savvy, but that language has many dialects. Some you need to know, some you don't, and some aren't invented yet. Here are some insights into the dialects and what you need to know about each.

Academese: The professional field of computer science has a language that is highly technical in nature and encompasses all the various segments of the field. For example, let's say John chooses to go into Computer Science. He gets an undergraduate degree and decides to go on to graduate school, specializing in Machine Learning. Once he decides on Machine Learning as a field, he can specialize further in Artificial Intelligence. Then John realizes that he is really interested in Natural Language Processing, again a subfield of AI. John now studies how computers process language by writing algorithms and processes that "teach" the computer to identify words and "tells" the computer what to do with them. That's pretty specific. While John probably has a basic understanding of how a database works, by this time he hasn't worked with one for a while and it would take him a while to build one and make it function well. And as for setting up his home wireless network, I'd be willing to bet my pharmacist neighbor knows more about that than John. In other words, you do not need to be a Computer Scientist in order to use and enjoy technology.

Programming: Our first computer was a TI99-4A. With 16K of memory we were all amazed at what it could do. When we added the peripherals box (disk drive and more memory), we were set! TI-Writer allowed us to format and print (on a dot matrix printer) but we had to exit the writing program and open a printing program to print, then exit the printing program and open TI-Writer to make changes or create another document. Formatting was limited to margins, bold, italic and underlining. But to do much more than that, you needed to learn how to program. So we did.

Simple hexadecimal programming codes could create graphics on the dot matrix printer. Add a little programming to the utilities and we could make the programs do more stuff. We were part of a support group because we desperately needed support to figure this stuff out. An added bonus of the support group was that many of them were actually programmers and so they shared the programs they created with dummies like us…which meant of course we got to reap the benefits of their work (which they saw as fun).

When the World Wide Web began to filter into the general public, the only way to create an online presence was to learn hypertext markup language (HTML) which coded the dots on the screen to create images. If you wanted a website, you had to learn HTML.

I am absolutely not a programmer. I absolutely am a power user, but I really wanted a website back in 1991. I learned HTML in order to put up a web page back when the Web was in its infancy, but believe me it was a lot of work. Then along came software that did the programming and formatting for you — WYSIWYG, or WhatYouSeeIsWhatYouGet — was my friend. HTML editors, and then website editing software, like Dreamweaver and Front Page, moved us farther from needing to know the programming codes. But we were still chained to our hardware and software to be able to upload and modify. Then came cloud computing....

Now, websites for social networking, social bookmarking and more have created online profile editors that are customizable, free, web-based and easy to use. A personalized website, via MySpace, Facebook, Xanga, Club Penguin and hundreds of others, is free and easy. Now updating or changing a website is just a click away. You can update from any computer, anywhere, anytime. Computing in the clouds (cyberspace).

The move away from having to learn specializing programming languages is now ingrained in the Web 2.0 culture. This means, for the casual user, no more obscure programming codes to learn and remember. So most of us will never need to learn any of it. Hooray!

Geekspeak: Language is a living organism, and as we encounter new events and experiences — technology-based and otherwise — they become incorporated into our language and thrive there. That's happened for centuries, and will continue to happen as our experiences increasingly are engaged in the online environment. These additions to our language style and form fall into two very distinct categories.

Terminology that defines either a thing or a process is one category. These are words that have made their way into our everyday language as a result of becoming comfortable with them as ubiquitous terms. We reach for a "Kleenex" or ask for a "Coke." A technology example might be that when we want to find out who wrote the novel *Moby Dick*, we "google" it. Google's search engine's language processing programming made finding things online so much easier it became the standard for web searches, hence replacing the term "search" with "google" and making what was only a noun both noun and verb. Others include URL (Uniform Resource Locater), Monitor, USB (Universal Serial Bus) and many more. A list of common terms and their definitions is in the glossary and online resources are available to track definitions as they change. Of course, our awareness and incorporation of this jargon is enhanced by our contact with it.

The second, Net lingo, comes out of the need to generate a sort of shorthand to increase typing speed by reducing the number of characters that need to be typed. These abound in chat rooms, message boards, and even email and are absolutely necessary when texting on miniscule cell phone keys. Acronyms like ROFL (rolling on the floor laughing) or TTYL (talk to you later) or BRB (be right back) are even making the crossover into spoken language among today's youth. Because youth are so much more engaged in the online culture (we'll talk about that later), frequently parents look at screens and have no idea how to follow the conversation, because it's an unfamiliar language. Just like spoken language, these will fall out of favor and new ones will be added, so it is imperative to be engaged in the culture in order to stay current. Again, we become more familiar with this language as we come into contact with it.

Hardware or Software: Like jargon, the machinery (hardware) or programmed tools (software) that are the physical manifestations of technology to most of us are constantly evolving. Smaller and smaller devices have larger and faster power to provide us with greater flexibility and mobility. More integrated functionality has eliminated much of the need to understand or provide special language prompts in order to make these work together.

The first computers had their own buildings in addition to their own language. Special cooling technology was created in order to keep it from overheating. Entire departments were created to work with and on these fussy and highly specialized monsters. Our family's first computer took up a very large desktop entirely. Finding space to put a piece of paper or book to type from was difficult. Setting it up and maintaining it was nearly a full-time job. Today, setting up a new computer is pretty easy. On-screen prompts and color-coded wires keep people like me, who are users and not hardware enthusiasts, from making too many mistakes.

Software, too, has made similar advances. Reflecting on our first days with word processing, it was cumbersome to use the software that seemed so cutting edge. We actually had to create a document in TI-Writer using hexadecimal codes for formatting and editing, save and close the file, then open the printing program and select the file to print. If we needed to make further changes, we had to close the print utility program and reopen the word processing program and file in order to make those changes using more codes, save again and close in order to reopen the print utility and re-print. Today's WYSIWYG (what-you-see-is-what-you-get) word processing editors allow you to manipulate text, add photos, format with thousands of typefaces and styles and print with the touch of a button to one of a cache of printers seems like child's play by comparison. Software installation setup programs guide you through step-by-step installation. New software provides not only comprehensive print manuals, but online support and in-program help features (like Word's annoying paperclip buddy). No coding required.

But hardware and software, too, have contributed to the language of technology in specific ways that you do need to be aware of when evaluating technology for purchase or upgrade. Understanding speed, internal memory for software and programs, memory for storage, portability, expandability, input and output options (like places for printers, drives, etc.) are critical to knowing whether the hardware will meet your needs.

And knowing what hardware you own is an absolute must to make sure the software you purchase will be compatible with it. There are two platforms: Mac and PC. There are various versions of operating systems on each and software is designed for specific platforms and operating systems. In other words, if you purchase software designed for a PC using Microsoft XP, it will not work on a PC using Microsoft Vista.

Note: Upgrading hardware almost always means upgrading software, a cost many forget to include!

I'm sure my neighbor and friend of years ago (she has long since moved away and we've lost touch) has bought a computer and probably upgraded it several times, giving in to the benefits technology gives us. Technology does and will continue to change and become better and more useful.

Does that mean upgrading to that new multi-media high-speed laptop you've seen advertised in last Sunday's ads? Maybe, maybe not. Does it mean little Johnny will be left out if he doesn't have the newest gaming console and web-enabled cell phone? I seriously doubt it.

CHAPTER FIVE

A Day in the Life of a Connected Teen

Susie is a 14-year-old girl and lives in Yourtown, USA, a small city with a mix of cultures and activities. She is an eighth-grader at Techno Middle School, which is a selective public school for students interested in math, technology and science.

She swims for her school and the local YWCA, is actively involved in her church youth group, and is involved in the school speech team on which she does original oratory.

Her parents, Millie and Fred, are average, hard-working, middle-income people who have been married now for 21 years. They like technology, and both have web-enabled cell phones because their work requires it. Millie is a sales representative for a textbook publisher, and Fred drives a delivery truck for a local furniture store. Susie is the third of their three children. Fred, Jr., the oldest, went off to the state college this year to study Forestry. Sally, the middle child, is always in her room creating something. She has won several art awards but her avant-garde dress and attitudes often put her at odds with her conservative family.

Let's listen in to a typical day for Susie.

6:35 AM: Susie wakes up and rolls over to her bedside table, swiping at it to capture her cell phone. She scrolls through her text messages, then gasps audibly and sits up.

Susie texts: OMG! Did josh realy cll u lst nyt? I wnt Dtails!

She punches some buttons, obviously listening to and deleting voice mails. Then she pushes some more buttons, taking the cell phone browser to Astrology.com. She reads: "It's going to be an awesome day! Take your smiles with you and enjoy!"

Mom calls to Susie: Bus in 20 minutes. Better put a move on!

8:10 AM: Susie is in her favorite class, Biology, pecking away on her ultra-mobile laptop. She is wirelessly connected to the Internet, as all are the students in her school, using the same equipment as required by school policy. The school does not forbid cell phones, but discourages the use of them during class hours unless they are specifically part of the instruction for that class. Susie, as well as all the other students, ignore the request to not use the phones to text throughout the day, and all are proficient at texting while the phone is in their pocket or backpack. In fact, Susie is texting Alicia, her best friend, about that phone call right now.

Susie: Dtails!

Alicia: i culdnt bleev it wen i lOkd @ caller id. u knw Ive had him n my favs 4 mths.

Susie: i knw. w@ tym wz it?

Alicia: aftr midnite. ph wz on vibr8 coz mom tAkz it awy f she hears it

Susie: me 2. w@ did he wnt

Alicia: he's havN a pRT fri nyt &he wnts me 2 cum. u cn cum 2

Susie: wow. my parNts wl nvr let me cum tho

Alicia: wanna tel em we're gunA d lib? dats w@ I'm gunA do.

Susie: gotta go. Mr. Simpson cmng dis wA. L8r

9:20 AM: In English Susie and her work group are working on creating a video blog about Shakespeare. Since Susie is on speech team, she's the group's unanimous choice to be the face and the voice for their project, an entry about *Othello*. Susie, Jason and Charlie are writing the script Susie will perform in front of her laptop webcam, Jen and Marty are downloading still images to show in between the video of Susie on their laptops. She can feel her phone vibrating in her pocket off and on, but she is so focused on writing and editing what she will say, she ignores it.

10:29 AM: Math today is about probability. Susie accesses the computer program that the students are to use, and downloads the pre-determined data set they are to use from the school's server. She is bored because she isn't interested in seeing what the probability is that one car will reach New York first starting from different points, going at different speeds, and so on. She sits in front of the computer, pecking the space bar occasionally to keep the screen saver from giving away that she is not working. Her fingers are furiously working on the keyboard on her phone, talking to Todd.

Susie: Im so bord. math cn B fun bt 2day jst lamo

Todd: heads ^. KP jst tld me there's a pop quiz n wrld hx

Susie: i'm K. read ll d asynmnts lst nyt. KV S wA Bhnd tho. btr tel her

Susie: cn we stdy sum @ lnch?

Susie: did KP giv u Ny specifics?

Todd: sry. txtN KV. jst sum topics coverd. nt ?

Susie: let's sit 2gtha @ lnch. txt JS n MK

Todd: K

11:15 AM: Susie, Todd, Justin, Marty, Kristen and Kyle are all eating salads. Three of them have their laptops open, searching for answers to the questions Kyle is telling them were on the quiz, and deciding which search "hits" to look through quickly. The other two are brainstorming answers and search terms to use to find answers they don't know. Occasionally, one or more of them pulls out their cell phone to check a text or phone call, but none of them answer calls although they respond sometimes to text messages.

12:45 PM: Susie is online again, taking an online pop quiz in her world history class. Each multiple-choice answer has a dot beside it to select the answer you want. Susie thinks, then clicks. Thinks again, then clicks again. She continues this throughout the quiz, then puts her headphones on when she is done and searches the school video site for the video they are to watch during the rest of the period. Her cell phone vibrates in her pocket throughout the hour.

1:25 PM: Susie is in Journalism class, editing video from the football games for the class DVD with Jerry. Actually, Jerry is doing the editing with comments here and there from Susie. Her cell phone buzzes in her pocket, telling her she has a new text message.

Mom: Susie, I will be late picking you up from practice. Can you get a ride home?
Susie: K. No prob
Mom: Thanx. Cya

2:30 PM: Health is Susie's last class of the day. Today the class has a guest speaker from the Department of Mental Health who is talking about how to recognize the signs of suicide. Right now, she is talking about how most suicides are the result of a very treatable condition: depression.

Speaker: "Suicide is very preventable, if we only know what to look for, and offer hope to those who see none."

Most of the class is listening politely. Two kids are snickering in the back of the room. Many of the students have their hands in their pockets.

3:45 PM: Swim practice means no access for two hours. Susie loves swimming laps, a different stroke each lap. Her cell phone buzzes off and on in the locker room. At the break, the coach starts off with assignments for relay teams. Allison isn't assigned to swim any relays, and has few spots in the coming meet, while Susie is selected for two relays and will be swimming three different events. Allison is obviously furious with Susie, and is staring holes through her. When practice ends, Susie takes her usual quick shower and gets in the car with Todd, who lives a block from her home.

9:45 PM: Susie has had dinner with her family, and is now reading a novel assigned for English class with her headphones in, listening to music. Every time her phone vibrates, she checks to see if she wants to answer. Frequently, she pecks in a text message. When Alicia texts, she put the book down.

Alicia: go 2 w3.flickr.com/photos/allisonw/susiek.asap
Susie: Y?
Alicia: jst GO

Susie clicks on Alicia's link, and starts screaming. Her mother, father and sister come running. She has her hand clasped tight over the phone, and her father has to pry it out of her hands. When he looks at the picture of his daughter in the shower after practice, he drops the phone in shock.

Their lives will never be the same.

CHAPTER SIX
The Education Connection

Knowledge is power, and access to knowledge gives us the power to change the world.

Parents are critical to our children's success in school. Research study after research study has clearly shown a strong correlation between parental involvement and academic success in elementary school, in middle school, and in high school. It is your responsibility to make sure your child understands that school is their job, and it is your responsibility as the consumer of the educational environment that the system is working at its highest level for your child. You are your child's best advocate.

But that means understanding the school's role as a public service to you and your child.

More than just providing them with tools and facts to use, the educational structure should be designed to prepare our children for success in whatever terms they ultimately decide to define it. In many ways, it is designed to help facilitate giving our children the tools, facts and opportunities to figure that for themselves and go for their goals. In a perfect world, parents, schools and communities should all be working together toward supporting youth in achieving at their highest potential.

Is that happening in every school, home and community? I wish. But it is working more often than it is not. Positive Youth Development research has come up with a variety of measures around what youth need to be successful. Two stand out.

The Search Institute has defined 40 Developmental Assets that all youth need in order to grow into caring, responsible adults. Their website (see Resources) breaks down the list into internal and external assets in a variety of social-emotional contexts. I highly recommend all those who work or live with youth in any way to become familiar with those assets and what they mean, in order to evaluate what support might be missing in the life of a youth to help him or her become wise, strong and successful.

America's Promise, started by General Colin Powell, defines 5 promises of wrap-around support that young people need for success in school, work and life. More information is available about this program at their website (see Resources).

- Caring Adults
- Safe Places
- A Healthy Start
- An Effective Education
- Opportunities to Help Others

All five of these promises are, in some way, part of what schools provide to students every day. They are staffed by caring adults, and even with recent school shootings schools are by far the safest place for children to be. School cafeterias provide good nutrition to many students for two meals a day. Many schools have a school nurse on site. Curriculum is constantly being re-searched and revised, and teachers upgrade their skills, and service-learning or leadership opportunities are available during both intra-curricular and extra-curricular activities.

Schools aren't just about reading, writing and 'rithmetic any more.

Digital Literacy

For centuries, literacy meant being able to read and write in a given language such as English or Spanish; digital literacy, however, does not at all mean being able to read and write in the language of technology — programming codes such as C++, PHP, etc. Moving beyond printed material that offers, in large part, pre-analyzed and contextualized content for us to digest, the sheer volume of resources online mean we must better able to analyze and contextualize information for ourselves in order to construct meaning. Critical thinking skills are ever more important in the smorgasbord of offerings presented to us online. David Warlick in *Redefining Literacy for the 21st Century* explains, "If all our children learn to do is read, they will not be literate."

We are not just readers and writers but participants in a very real and tangible way...clicking our way through links to either get lost in the morass of possibilities or get to where we wanted to go. Or uploading video taken with our cell phone cameras or commenting on a friend's social networking profile or adding our two cents worth to a Wikipedia entry we think needs it. Authority is being democratized every time a picture, a comment, a video, a podcast, and more is posted on any website or forum. The web is giving voice to people, especially youth, who have been marginalized or even ignored since the inception of a social structure, unless they gathered in mobs and demanded attention.

So what exactly does it mean to be literate in today's high tech world? What will it mean to be an educated person for the 21st Century? Here's my definition:

Digital Literacy is the ability to access, acquire, decode, evaluate, synthesize, organize and communicate information in multiple formats from a wide range of sources which may be presented through any medium – audio, visual, print or electronic.

In other words, successful adults need to be able to *access* — know how to reach information stored on library shelving or jump drives, *acquire* — open books or files, *evaluate* — make a determination of validity or value for the purpose, *synthesize* — construct meaning from that information, *organize* — arrange in a logical order that suits the purpose, and *communicate* — share the constructed knowledge in a clear and concise manner to others. No small task for the education community of today, or for their students.

Obsolescence and Access

I was at a higher education conference for teachers of writing, being held on a large state university campus. One of the breakout sessions got into a discussion of whether knowing how to access electronic information — work the computer it was stored on — might be part of being literate. The audience was split, and a rousing discussion ensued.

A faculty member from the host university told us about one of the student computer labs at the time. The lab had about a dozen computers, all of which were either different platforms (Mac or PC) or had very different operating systems and versions of software. For the students, that meant being able to work on—being literate in—nearly a dozen machines. She thought this was horrible. Several others thought it helped guarantee that the students were more flexible in their ability to access information. There was never a consensus. There still isn't in the education community.

At any rate, technology brings with it change, and adults are not great at getting on board, seeing the relevance and opportunity that technology brings with it. And professional educators are possibly less likely to see the relevance and opportunity than those faced with keeping a business viable. Just the way it is.

This isn't just a recent phenomenon. Schools have been slow to adopt and adapt to teaching with and through technological tools for a long, long time.

Take for example what happened to me in high school. I wanted to take typing because I loved to write but hated the manual method of holding a pencil and scribbling (and I do mean scribbling...to this day my handwriting is atrocious) over yellow lined pages. My high school, however, discouraged me from taking typing as it was not a college-bound class and I was in the college-bound track. No matter the benefit it might bring me by making my writing legible to myself and others—this use of an existing device was limited in relevance to those in the "Business Ed" classes who were not destined for college and careers. That typing might at the time or in the future be relevant to anyone else was beyond the imagination of my school administrators. Fortunately, I had a mother who advocated for me...and I took at against the repeated and ridiculous admonitions that I might chuck the idea of college if I knew how to operate a typewriter.

Today, I can't say for certain if I would have graduated from college, and almost certainly would not have become a professional writer and teacher of writing, if I had not taken typing in night classes (they refused to let me in as part of my regular schedule). I am absolutely positive I wrote longer papers in college, edited and revised them more thoughtfully, and generally took writing more seriously because I could type.

Typing made writing possible for me in a way I cannot completely describe or explain. I just know today, and knew then at 15, that this was a technology that could change my world for the better. And now with the benefit of hindsight, I know that it has and continues to do so as new technologies make editing and revising ever more available on smaller and more portable devices. How much more easily I adapted to working on a computer keyboard than many of my peers. And today…knowing how to type is a prerequisite for success even in elementary settings!

Those school counselors and administrators feared learning a new technology would change who I was and who I wanted to be. Obviously, it did not. I don't think technology changes WHO we are (and I don't think it ever will), but I absolutely believe it is changing HOW we interact…the intricate mechanisms of our relationship with each other and with the world through an anytime-anywhere series of connections and opportunities. Social Networking sites are redefining the word "friend" as teenagers share their deepest fears and highest hopes with hundreds of people they've accepted as their online friends, many of which they've never met in person...and never will. And that's okay.

All that Glitters

As a teacher and instructional designer, I am very conservative as I design the technological elements for an online course. If you can't prove to me there is a positive outcome for technological glitz in a course...it doesn't belong! More technology does not necessarily mean better education. However, no technology does mean an inadequate education, and fortunately there are many educators out there who agree with me and are trying to integrate technology into learning and facilitate learning with it.

But what many educators, particularly those over the age of 30, fail to realize is that technology shouldn't be taught as a separate subject to the digital natives. To our youth, technology is a fluid part of their lives — weaving in and out as part of the F2F world seamlessly and effortlessly as they communicate, plan, entertain and are entertained.

That's the way we need to be teaching those digital natives; the technology, the student and the material can dictate how, when, if, what technology will blend into the F2F classroom environment seamlessly, effortlessly, jointly. The days of the separate computer lab as a way to integrate technology into teaching is past. That is not to say that focused time in computer lab environments, and focused time without technology available at all is part of a bygone era. Both are still valid strategies for facilitating learning. But the notion that technology is a tool, as I discussed in Chapter 3, to be pulled out, dusted off and used occasionally, simply must go away.

This is just as true in your homes as it is in our schools. We as parents need to be advocating for and supporting the school's efforts to reach the goal of truly embedding technology — all technology — into how we teach and learn, becoming as natural a part of good instruction as a textbook or magazine is considered today. Our digital natives are doing it without us anyway.

Distance Learning

I was asked to develop and teach the English 101-102 Freshman Composition sequence in a completely virtual environment. I had fought it for quite a while, even though I was working with faculty to design and implement web-centric and web-enhanced courses in several other disciplines at the time, for some reason I resisted teaching my own courses online. The time came that I was traveling so much that I could no longer guarantee that I could actually show up at a F2F class, so I dove in and launched Virtual 101, meeting the first day with the class in the assigned classroom because they all thought they had signed up for a F2F class. None were disappointed, however, because their first thought was that they never had to show up for that 8am class again!

I'll never forget the first semester. I had one student who had left her rural, Eastern Kentucky town for the first time, and was literally terrified of computers, and terrified of living in the "Big City" of Lexington, Kentucky. She came to me on the first day and confessed her fears, but said if I would work with her she would give online a shot. I promised her I would help and assured her she could do it. At the end of the semester, she wrote me an email I have framed that said of all the faculty she worked with that semester (mine was the only online course) I was the only one who cared whether she passed or not. High Tech can indeed be High Touch!!

Distance Learning classes, in whatever format they are taught (compressed video, web-enhanced, web-centric, etc.) are completely different animals than their F2F counterparts. The differences a virtual classroom offers can be both benefits and drawbacks.

- Anywhere access to education no matter how remote the location
- Small schools can provide classes in which perhaps only one student is interested
- Students can do work on different time schedules
- Students who are uncomfortable speaking out tend to be more assertive with less risk
- Students have 24/7 contact to class materials, work, classmates and instructor

- Technology documents conversation and discussion accessible 24/7
- Technology documents assignment deadline verification
- Students tend to procrastinate by waiting til deadline to begin
- Gradebooks are available to track progress 24/7
- Much distance learning is poorly designed and tries to replicate the classroom environment
- Many classes limited to "Kill and Drill" workbook-style instruction
- Feedback on wrong answers is often missing
- Others can do the online assignments for students enrolled (not a new phenomenon)

Distance learning, although it's been around for several decades, is still in its infancy. In order to really provide an interactive, engaging online environment for students, technology is going to have to move a little farther along, particularly in the area of video. However, excellent education is just as available online as it is offline. Not all teachers are cut out to teach online, and not all students are cut out to perform well in the online environment either. For teachers, the online environment is more time-consuming and requires more relationship-building. For students, the online environment takes greater dedication to task and more interactivity.

Great distance learning, like great education of any kind, requires a lot of preparation, a lot of thought, a lot of time, and a lot of caring interaction both faculty to student and student to student.

Context, Validity and Communication

When I was fairly young, someone told me that "Being educated doesn't mean knowing all the facts, it means knowing where to go to get the facts." That made so much sense to me at the time, and makes even more sense to me today as the sheer volume of information becomes more and more evident with age. But in a world where we can resolve trivia questions by punching a few buttons on our cell phones as we eat dinner out, does the ready availability of information mean that we are all magically educated individuals? I think not.

Being educated means not only getting the facts, but also knowing how to put them in a context that is useful and makes sense for us in our lives. Ahhhh. There's the rub.

This new Web 2.0 world provides, for the first time, a completely uncensored and uncontextualized resource. Think about it. Newspapers have editors, television shows have censors, little media is truly "live" because there is that 3-second delay. All previous types of media resources have had somebody sitting back in the shadows, deciding what we got to see and what we didn't. And we weren't taught, in the decades prior to 1990, how to sift through item after item of multi-media unevaluated content in order to find credible, useful and authoritative information for our needs.

And we certainly weren't taught (and before 1990 as a composition instructor I had no need to teach) how the formatting of a paper, choice of font, color, or graphics impacted the message my students were asked to create for their essays. All we really needed to know was to keep the left side straight and either double or single-space and proofread, proofread, proofread. Communication is impacted by presentation, but presentation can severely get in the way of effective communication.

I wish Marshall McLuhan could've seen the fourth-graders at a conference where I recently spoke, pumped up and wiggly as fourth-graders on display will be, demonstrate for the 700 participants how they created, in groups, PowerPoint presentations on science topics instead of writing the traditional report on paper. I can't say they learned a thing about their topics or the science behind them, but I know for sure they learned all about how to make things dance, jump and rotate onscreen, fly in, fade in or wipe in, the colors, sizes and shapes of various fonts, and how what rap song (usually copyrighted) fourth-graders think goes best with a presentation on the social habits of bees, for example. In this case, the medium obscured the message.

Obviously, there is a good deal more to using technology well than just providing access. The proliferation of personal websites and the graphic design horrors many of them exhibit are a testament to the fact that society today still isn't doing a great job at learning those skills.

Essentially, we need to:

- Understand what a search engine is and how it works
  - o Navigation
  - o Bookmarking
  - o Keywords
  - o Link Heirarchy and advertising
- Know what kinds of questions to ask to find what you want
- Identify the type and role the resources found might play
- Be able to scan resources rather than read line-by-line at first
- Evaluate resources as they pertain to your criteria for resources to meet your need
- Evaluate resources for authority and credibility
- Understand how to use that information without plagiarizing

- Blend information from multiple sources into a knowledge base useable for you
- Communicate that knowledge to others, using only those features (font, graphics, motion) that enhance your message. In this case, less is more.

Evaluating web content really isn't any different from evaluating any resource. For decades teachers have been asking students to consider the five Ws of research:

1. Who — publishes it
2. What — credentials do they bring to the information
3. Where — can I find more about the topic
4. When — was the information last updated
5. Why — should I believe what they offer

There is much more to consider in terms of using technology responsibly and safely in educational environments, but that is covered more thoroughly in the next chapter. Cybersafety is a critical piece of helping our children learn to live with all these opportunities without putting themselves, and their communities, at risk.

So, as parents who want to and need to work collaboratively with the school your child attends, it is your responsibility to ensure that your child is paying attention and cooperating with the school in its efforts to facilitate his or her learning. And it is your responsibility to ensure that you are getting what you are paying for as a consumer of the education system in America — a young person who is enjoying learning more about himself and the world around him.

Because your tax dollars are paying for it with every tax dollar deducted from each paycheck, and in so many more ways.

CHAPTER SEVEN
Cyber-Safety

There are guys that wear black hats and guys that wear white ones. Sometimes, in the virtual world, as in the F2F world, it's hard to tell the difference.

Okay, I'll say it. The Internet is not safe. Is the F2F world safe? The same people — both good and evil — that populate the physical world populate the virtual world. Just as we work to keep kids safe in the physical world, we need to work at making the virtual world just as safe as possible. But convincing yourself that by denying access to a computer or website to a child — when easy, free access is all around us — is all you have to do to make them safe is foolhardy.

Do you let your child out the door every morning? Of course you do. How could they learn to live in the world if you didn't? The same question — and answer — applies to the Internet. It truly is an integrated part of the world in which we live.

The reality is that about 90% of those that inhabit the virtual world are responsible citizens, making good choices and being considerate of others. This is true in the physical world, and so it is true in the virtual world. While bad guys are out there, and they are indeed looking for your posts and information, the bad guys are not the majority of online citizens. We are.

The 2008 Pew Internet Project study showed that of youth ages 12-19:

- 94% are researching school assignments, 48% daily
- 81% go to websites about movies, TV shows, music groups, sports star
- 64% upload user-created content
- 35% of teen girls blog, while 20% of boys blog (new blog every second)
- Nearly 50% of teens have posted photos online
- 54% of wired girls post photos, while 40% of boys do
- Nearly 20% of boys have posted a video, compared to 10% of girls

Parents need to become aware of technology policies that schools have in place, becoming aware of how these policies and disciplinary actions may affect your children, as well as making sure that they are as up-to-date and sensible as they should be.

Find out if your school has:

- An Acceptable Use Policy that connects misuse to disciplinary actions that are logical for the abuse. For example, barring Johnny from using school technology for creating a derogatory social networking profile of Sally won't teach him not to do it from a friend's house.

- A school-wide bullying prevention program that encourages respect and bystander action.

- A clear connection between behavior and consequences either online or offline in the code of conduct. The Internet doesn't have boundaries, and online behavior done off-campus clearly impacts the school climate.

- Regular professional development and support for teachers to develop and use technology in creative, authentic, and engaging ways in their classrooms.

Years of being around prosecution and law enforcement have confirmed for me that there really ARE predators out there looking for your little Johnny or Joanna online. We really do need to be concerned and we need to know what information is being put out there by our kids not only about them — but by them about US! This chapter looks at common misconceptions and thought patterns that put families at risk and can create barriers to positive, proactive parenting both online and offline.

Both youth and adults have adopted belief systems about technology that misguide and placate…putting both youth and their entire communities at risk. I commonly come across these attitudes as I travel about, speaking to adults and youth about responsible digital citizenship for both. In an age where more knowledge is available to us all faster than we've ever been able to access it…it is amazing what we don't know! Or perhaps it's what we just don't want to know because it might force us to reevaluate our behavior? Hmmmm.

I've grouped these myths and misunderstandings about the virtual safety issues into five categories which I feel best represent the most dangerous and most widely represented myths and misunderstandings:

1. Myth—The Internet gives the perception that whatever is posted is both temporary and under the complete control of the person posting. Whether a profile is private or not (and certainly if it's private) no one will see it except for those they want to see it. There are websites where information that is housed is completely safe. I only post things my friends can see.

2. Myth—Updated technology has considered safety hazards of earlier systems and therefore is safer. Technology people are constantly working to make websites safer to protect their audience's information and person.

3. Myth—While there really are socially-deficient people out there who prey on unfortunate children, we know who lives in our neighborhoods and we have taught our kids about stranger danger. That happens, but it happens in other neigh-

borhoods to other peoples' children. Some research even says the media hype is overblown.

4. Myth—Let's face it, kids will be kids. They can be nasty to each other but after all, what doesn't kill us makes us stronger, right? We have all been tested by the fire, and we all survived. These kids will too. Besides, some people are just sooooo touchy. I was JK—Just Kidding!

5. Myth—My family knows not to post our social security numbers, home phone numbers, birthdates or addresses online. As long as we keep private information to ourselves, we are safe.

Here are my responses to each myth or misunderstanding, gleaned from lengthy and numerous discussions with programmers, web developers, law enforcement, prosecution, victims and perpetrators. The examples are just a sampling of what has really happened. The negative impact on our physical world as a result of misbehaviors and misconceptions is the focus of much media attention and many parent conversations.

In my opinion, the fault lies with the myths and misconceptions which allow and encourage irresponsible behavior, more than with the technology. If you drive drunk, you are more likely to have a serious, possibly fatal, accident. Is that crash the fault of the alcohol producer or is it your fault? The analogy translates well to this situation.

The Forever Rule

The Internet is neither temporary nor under your control. Everything is archived somewhere by someone—FOREVER. "Private" profiles are easily hacked. Go to Google and search using the term "Hacking MySpace" and you get step-by-step instructions to hack a profile, as well as instructions on how to close the programming hole. But for each programming fix, another hole is found. There is no such thing as a totally "safe" website, just like there is no physical location that is completely and totally safe. Actions that are funny to a 13-year-old may seem less so when that youth turns 40 and has to explain to a spouse or a supervisor what he was thinking at the time. What goes up today is there FOREVER!

For example, take the case of the Millersville University student in Pennsylvania who posted a picture on her social networking profile. The picture had her wearing a pirate's hat—Millersville University's mascot is the Marauder—and drinking from an opaque glass. She was of legal drinking age at the time, and although she claims she was not drinking alcohol, she decided to put the caption "Drunken Pirate" under the photo. The picture allegedly appeared while she was completing her student teaching internship for a degree in education and teaching certificate for Pennsylvania. The University has all students sign an "Acceptable Use Policy" which apparently said they could be disciplined for inappropriate or unprofessional behavior. The student was not allowed to graduate with a degree in education, and was considered ineligible for a Pennsylvania teaching certificate.

I have met many students who have failed classes, changed majors, lost internships, and been turned down for scholarships and positions due to online material posted because it was "Just for Friends." That was not a defense that held water for those making the decisions. This woman's case will be documented forever on thousands of websites, and her legal battle to become certified followed by thousands more. Her future has been changed — FOREVER.

The Cell Phone Dilemma

The overarching philosophy here is one posed earlier in the book — match the technology to the need. Evaluate the benefit and potential harm. Brainstorm possible unintended outcomes.

Most digital natives have landlines only if they need a DSL connection for Internet access. It's rare to find a college student with a landline any more. Parents feel more secure in an ever-more-threatening world if 10-year-old Becky can reach Mom anytime, anywhere. And because Mom has a cell phone number programmed into Becky's phone, she is free to go to lunch with friends, shop, run errands or head to the gym.

But what happens to all those cell phones we upgrade every year or two? Last month at 3:00am our phone rang (landline…we have DSL). When I picked up, a male voice said, "Doris?" I said yes, and the young man's voice asked what I was up to. I asked who it was, and he said "Johnny." Matter-of-Fact. Like I should know who he was. The conversation didn't get any better...actually went toward the obscene pretty quickly...and I asked how he got this number and my name. His answer blew me away! He had gotten a loaner phone from AT&T and it had all these numbers programmed into it with names...including mine. He was calling them all to see if he could hook up. I couldn't wait til the offices opened in the morning to call and complain!

When parents really understand negative consequences of TXTing, video bullying, school bombings (many bombs are set to go off at cell frequencies), and privacy issues, they agree that cell phones are a privilege rather than a right...and frequently more of a boondoggle than a boon. Armed with that knowledge and belief system, the age-old "but everyone is doing it" goes out the window.

Web-enabled video or camera cell phones I consider particularly insidious in the hands of those under about age 24. The FOREVER damage that can be done at a party by one tipsy and therefore less inhibited adolescent or college student is irreversible and instantly global.

Text messaging is a permanent record, and you can access each and every text your child sends. Some carriers have this capability available for parents, some may require software to access it. I highly recommend every once in a while you pick up your child's phone and look at the pictures, emails, call log and texts that have been sent from it.

Let me say again that online access is not something that is optional however. Today's youth have a social life that is fully integrated into both the physical and virtual worlds. They use social networking and texting to enhance and expand their F2F lives, and use F2F opportunities to expand and enhance their virtual lives. Adults only know, for the most part, how to do the former.

The Cyber-Predator and Pornography

The Internet has facilitated the spread of pornography and created easy connections to children, youth and adults for those who prey on others. According to federal statistics, child pornography had been pretty much eliminated by the early 1990's through global co-operation with postal systems. The Web, particularly Web 2.0, has created a proliferations of sites and distribution bringing the problem of child pornography to epic proportions.

Providing a protective and mitigating presence in the online world helps parents sort out what to look for, how to document a potential threat, and when, how and to whom these things can and should be reported.

I spent a stomach-turning two hours or so at a national law enforcement conference about a year ago in the portable FBI Child Pornography Lab, looking at pictures of child pornography (with blurred faces et al.) helping to identify items in the picture that might lead law enforcement to identify the date or location that the picture was taken. I was able to get through them because I felt I might be helping to locate a child, and the predator, and stop it.

But what is even more frightening is that teenagers and younger children are now part of the pornography business. Some are willingly taking sexually explicit pictures of themselves and others, then posting them to profiles or texting them to friends. Predators are trolling these sites for just such pictures to copy and include in their collections, as well as to identify potential victims. Why? I haven't a clue. But it's really happening. I was upgrading my PDA recently and got to talking about it with my cell service representative. He told me horror stories about seeing pornographic pictures on children's cell phones when he was asked to upgrade their phones. Companies need to be setting policies about when to contact law enforcement in these situations.

JK (Just Kidding)

Words do hurt. And words or pictures posted online that we have no control over hurt way more.

Bullying is growing in our society. It's bad in the physical world and research says adults generally don't notice it to intervene; it's much worse in the virtual world where adults aren't even there to see it. Mental Health providers explain that bullying is a loss experience: loss of safety, loss of self-esteem, loss of belonging and a loss of a sense of control over your own life.

These losses can build up, and lead to another loss — loss of life. I work frequently with Mark Neblett, who lost his daughter Rachel to suicide after she was severely bullied both F2F and online. Her family has created an organization to help prevent any other youth from choosing suicide as an answer to pain. While Rachel's school, parents, and friends were supportive and worked with mental health officials and trainers to help Rachel, ultimately the depression that built as a result of the losses she felt overcame her. Rachel is just one of many children who are overcome. I hope you agree with me that one child is too many to lose.

Bullying prevention in school and in society requires buy-in from every adult in the organization in order to be effective. School-wide discipline and behavior expectations must be re-evaluated and clearly, consistently, fairly enforced.

The Olweus Bullying Prevention Program is considered somewhat of the gold standard of bullying prevention programming. There are many more programs available that include or expand upon that program. But most everyone agrees about the definition of bullying:

> *"Bullying occurs when a person is exposed repeatedly and over time, to negative actions on the part of one or more students." Dan Olweus*

The definition of cyber-bullying from the president of Bullying.org is somewhat different, but largely the same:

> *"Cyber-Bullying involves the use of information and communication technologies… to support deliberate, repeated, and hostile behavior by an individual or group, that is intended to harm others." –Bill Belsey*

One more thing. Conflict resolution is NOT bullying prevention. While it has its place, it has been proven over and over to be ineffective as a bullying prevention process. Don't even think that bringing two kids together to "work it out and shake hands as friends" means that once those same two kids that shook hands in the principal's office will turn the corner down the hall and remain "friends."

Identity Theft

The Federal Trade Commission reports that young people make up 31% of reported cases of identity theft each year., and the 12-21 age group is the largest growing demographic for identity theft. Social Networking sites are in the news as the technology of choice for gathering personal information.

As I research and surf social networking sites, I find amazing amounts of personal information that can be aggregated to provide what we know to be "private" information. Casual conversation with an online "friend" can provide clues to age, sex, location — the tools of the ID thief's trade. Ask any 14-year-old what ASL means, and they'll blurt out: Age, Sex, Location.

That's the first question posed when you enter any chat room.

It's hard for children to distinguish between personal information that could be harmful and personal information that isn't. Talk to your children about how conversations about winning a game, your team's mascot and colors, who your friends are, favorite restaurants and shops, and more can lead to a dossier of information many spies would be envious of.

Cyber-Security

There are strategies and tools to know when and how to instigate higher levels of protection without getting bogged down in the highly technical. While this could be an entire chapter in and of itself, these strategies and tools are changing as fast as the technology it is designed to help us with.

Do security tools give a false sense of security to parents? I find that for the most part, parents want a simple and quick fix that does make them feel better, and security tools offer that. Just like a metal detector at the courthouse or school door is designed to keep out guns, explosives and knives, a security device is designed to keep out intruding viruses, predators, etc. But either are subject to creative minds who can, if they really want to, find a way to beat the system.

However, most of us lock our doors at night, even though law enforcement has shown us repeatedly that if a criminal really wants into your house, they will figure out a way to get past that locked door. But the reality is, as law enforcement goes on to say, that most criminals aren't after *your* house, they're just after *someone's* house. So the more barriers you present, the more likely that criminal will go after an easier mark. The same is true with your computer and your online information.

In my opinion, the best security is an adult *Being There, Being Aware* and *Being the Parent*. The more knowledgeable you are as a parent about what your computer, or your child, is doing, the better able you are to create a safe and secure environment with information to guide responsible decisions about behavior, with tools that address specific known problems, and with software that help nip potential problems in the bud.

Security software and hardware selections and types change dramatically from day to day and as technology continues to advance. Because of that, I recommend taking this basic information to your local computer store and talking to them about the financial, technical knowledge and time commitment involved. Just like you should match your technology to your lifestyle needs, match the security and safety technology you use to your lifestyle requirements. For example, I wouldn't be without encrypted wireless in my home, but because it is now just the two of us, a keystroke capture isn't necessary. Now if grandchildren arrive, you can be sure that is one of the first things I'll install before a visit!

Top 5 Free and Easy Safety/Security Tools

1. Put the computer in a public place where it is clearly visible and walk by frequently silently
2. Establish family rules for time online, signing on, behavior expectations and consequences
3. Use the tools that come with all computers: passwords, browser history, cookies, proxy checks,

firewalls and get help if you don't know how to check these on your specific computer or browser software from any computer store

4. If you have wireless and laptops, establish when and where they can be used

5. Have each family member write down userid and password for each site they join which is to be kept in a sealed/signed envelope in their room where you can access it if something happens

Safer Surfing Internet Tips

1. Monitor and limit excessive web use, keeping computers in easily visible areas

2. Learn about the key technologies used

3. Teach kids about proper web use and "netiquette"

4. Encourage discussion about web use and alert adults of any issues

5. Speak with school about any issues, and go to the police if threat is made

6. Save and print any cyberbully messages

7. Discontinue communication with any bullying or threatening online "friend"

Monitoring Online Use

1. Google each family member's name at least twice a year (and every nickname)

2. Online activity (checking the web for information about your family)

3. Keystroke Capture Devices (most effective and range from free to $100)

4. Proxy Software (requires fairly high technology expertise and easily bypassed)

5. Filtering Software (often filters appropriate as well as inappropriate content)

6. Human Oversight (just walking by or around is the least effective method)

CHAPTER EIGHT
The Learning Spiral

What goes around keeps going.

Years ago I heard someone say that we had surpassed the Learning Curve and have moved into a Learning Spiral. I still quote that repeatedly; I believe it is the perfect analogy for the movement of a world blessed (and cursed) with an ever-expanding, ever-changing advent of technology growth. The Internet is really all about the opportunity for each and every one of us to have access to knowledge and information instantly, as we need it. Our world is poised at a point with technology for incredible richness, rigor and wonder. The wide access technology affords makes this possible in a way community libraries of just books provided in a much more limited and yet more contextualized and content-edited manner.

With this wide resource of rewards comes a very real and present risk. It's time for the generation charged with building the policies for this rapid and challenging growth to come out of our comfort zones and begin dealing with this as a reality.

Every time I provide a professional development workshop or give a keynote I am still surprised with the reactions. Many in the audience come up to me afterwards and tell me how much they learned and how overwhelmed they are with fear. My goal is never to scare people — it is to motivate them to act by facing the realities of what is happening, both good and evil, on the Internet right now.

And every time I give a presentation to students, I am similarly surprised by the two very different reactions I get from them. Half of them are incensed that I got on their profiles (I have never had to do any hacking) and downloaded things they posted "Just for my friends." The other half come up to shake my hand and tell me they are deleting their profiles that evening. That isn't my goal either.

Youth today need to learn how to use these technologies safely, responsibly, and well in order to be competitive in the world they are preparing to enter. But in order to learn to become responsible, caring adults, they need parents who can *Be There, Be Aware,* and *Be the Parent.* That means being responsible, caring parents who take seriously the roles of modeling appropriate behavior in all the places youth inhabit, mentoring their children as they learn to navigate the choices that will lead them to reach their goals, and monitoring their behavior to be able to respond by intervening to keep them safe or by rewarding responsible behavior.

There are those parents that believe that parents looking at children's sites erodes trust between parents and youth. My husband and I do not ascribe to that mindset. Law enforcement research indicates that there is a 3-6 hour window to find a child alive if abducted. Precious minutes tick by as law enforcement and you try to figure out where to look. Most digital natives have clues if not outright directions to potential locations on social networking sites. You want to be able to access them instantly. The same is true of many teen suicide victims. You have the opportunity to be that "fly on the wall" to keep your child safe through monitoring their online experiences like you monitor their activities in the physical world.

My husband and I feel very strongly about our role as teacher, mentor, role model and monitor in the lives of our children. Being aware of decisions our children were making, whether we disagreed with them or not, gave us opportunities for conversation and relationship-building. Some gave us "teachable moments" where we were able to share our perspective on the potential harm these decisions might bring to our child or our family or others. Those "unintended consequences" that youth and adults frequently miss altogether can be looked at and considered openly and freely in the light of awareness.

Rules of Thumb

- Create an open dialogue with youth to talk about their activities on the Internet and create rules for computer use. Be consistent in enforcing these rules.

- Adults and youth use computers in different ways for different things. Engage youth as your teacher in what's available online that you don't know about.

- Put home and school computers with Internet access in a visible location where you can monitor activities. Screens between students and teachers create an educational barrier.

- Surf the Internet with your child and discuss where the child likes to go and what they like to do. Use this time to educate your child on the dangers of visiting inappropriate sites, opening unknown emails/messages, befriending virtual acquaintances and giving out personal information online.

- Help your child create accounts/profiles on social networking sites and know the password to any account he/she creates, just as you reserve the right to go into their room in your house. Also, create your own account on any social networking site (i.e. MySpace, Xanga, Facebook) and mandate your child to add you as a friend. This gives you access to your child's personal web pages and activities.

- Periodically search for your name, your child's name (and nicknames) and their friends through Google, MySpace, Facebook, Xanga, Bebo and others to monitor activity by or about yourself and your family.

- Activate or buy software or navigational programs that limit your child's Internet use. Remember that software does not take the place of adult guidance.

- Tell your child never to give out personal information to anyone, such as name, age, birthday, school name, city, phone number, picture and other identifying information, and be cautious about information provided in casual conversation online. Have a discussion about what information might lead to being identified. Be sure all accounts are set to "private," although also realize privacy settings are easily hacked.

- Tell your child never to meet face-to-face with someone they met on the Internet unless they have your permission, and tell you right away if any online comments or activities make them uncomfortable.

- Inform local law enforcement, school or Internet Service Provider (ISP) when you or your child is concerned about bullying, Internet threats or illegal activity.

Online Resources

Web 2.0 Information Websites
www.youtube.com/watch?v=pMcfrLYDm2U
www.youtube.com/watch?v=ljbI-363A2Q&feature=related
www.youtube.com/watch?v=6gmP4nk0EOE
http://www.pbs.org/wgbh/pages/frontline/shows/teenbrain/
http://www.pbs.org/wgbh/pages/frontline/kidsonline
fairuse.stanford.edu

Internet Safety Websites
www.netsmartz.org
www.wiredsafety.org
www.ncpc.org
http://www.familywatchdog.us/
http://www.fbi.gov/fbikids.htm
www.safekids.org
www.nsopw.gov
www.ncmec.org
www.mcgruff.org
www.safetyclicks.com
www.isafe.org
www.bully.org
www.bullyfree.com
www.bullybeware.com
www.backoffbully.com
www.antibullying.net
www.peerabuse.info
www.safekids.org
www.stopbullyingnow.org
www.stopcyberbullying.org
www.cyberbullying.us
http://www.commonsensemedia.org/internet-safety

Social Networking Websites
www.myspace.com
www.facebook.com
www.secondlife.com
www.bebo.com

Gaming Websites
www.worldofwarcraft.com
www.runescape.com
www.maplestory.com
www.rockstargames.com/IV

Check These Out! Websites
www.googleearth.com
www.ed.gov/about/offices/list/os/technology
www.eschoolnews.com
www.smithsonianeducation.org/
www.microsoft.com/Education
www.thinkfinity.org/
http://www.shine.com
http://www.zoeysroom.com
www.craigslist.org
www.petfinders.org
www.wikipedia.com
www.disney.com
www.nickelodeon.com

Specialized Community Websites
www.fawm.org
www.pogo.com
www.ourstage.com
www.photoblog.com
www.snapfish.com
www.friendster
www.fanfic.com
www.kazaa.com

www.flipdrive.com
www.twitter.com
www.flickr.com
www.photobucket.com
www.youtube.com
www.xanga.com
www.clubpenguin.com
www.webkinz.com
www.livejournal.com
www.blogger.com
www.delicious.com
www.digg.com

Positive Youth Development Sites
www.search-institute.org
www.americaspromise.org
www.pbis.org
www.dropoutprevention.org

Glossary of Terms

ASL: This is the first thing you are asked when you enter a chat room, and it stands for Age, Sex, Location. These are also the prime information needed for identity thieves.

ASP: This type of programming allowed web developers to begin to really make websites dynamic, or be able to change according to what the user needed. Also called creating content "on the fly" or as the user set parameters to tell the site what he/she was interested in. Usually set up in a database of some sort, the user selects from choices that draw from the database in order to create a user-specific page.

BLOG: Originally called a WebLog, the term has been shortened to just Blog. Essentially, it is an online journal or diary.

Digital: Most commonly used in electronics or computing, it refers to converting discrete information into binary numeric form that computers can read.

Digital Native: Someone born before 1987, generally speaking.

DRAM: Dynamic random access memory (DRAM) is a type of memory that stores data in a separate circuit. The circuit needs to be recharged periodically in order to keep working, so it is dynamic memory as opposed to static memory.

F2F: Face to Face, or F2F in text lingo, is a synonym for the physical world in which we live.

Flash Drive: Generally a USB device, it is a new type of memory stick that allows larger amounts of data to be stored on little bitty drive sticks. Otherwise known as thumb drives.

Geek: General term for someone who likes technology a lot. It could be someone who likes to work with hardware, likes programming, or just is a power user of technology.

Geekspeak: All the terms here, and many, many more.

Internet: The hardware that is all joined together to create the World Wide Web. There are thousands of servers across the world that connect to allow access to the Web.. That's why it's called the Web.

IM: Instant Messaging has been around since the early 1990s. Every site has it's own version of IMing.

Leet Speak—Also known as hakspeak, leetspeak is a type of communications where a user replaces letters for numbers or other characters. For example, "leet" in leetspeak would become "1337". Below is our basic conversion tool to convert your text into leetspeak. Please keep in mind there are hundreds of different ways that someone may speak leet; therefore, someone may use "5" or a "$" to represent an "S".

MHz—the internal processing speed of your hardware, or how fast things can go. Again, the faster your processor, the more things can be open and working. But the more that is open, the slower the computer goes no matter how fast your processor is.

Netlingo: Language that has evolved out of internet use. Generally referred to as text lingo as well, it is similar to Leet Speak.

Optical mouse: A computer mouse drives the little arrow, or cursor, on your monitor . Some of them have little balls that get dirty and cause the mouse not to work well. An optical mouse uses a light sensor rather than a ball.

P2P: A Peer-to-Peer network allows sharing of files directly from computer to computer without posting on a website. This was how music files were swapped illegally.

Perl: Another programming language.

Phishing: Identity thief scams that come via email generally, imitating your bank or credit card company, asking you to click somewhere to verify your secure information. You click, you're history. Lots of emails from Nigerian folks trying to transfer large sums into your bank account as well. Don't do it.

PHP: Another programming code used by web developers.

RAM: This determines how many things you can have open and functioning well at a time. Run out of RAM and you run out of computing space.

SRAM: Static memory that has a permanent spot in your computer's memory to store information.

TXT: Text Messaging, or TXTing, is the common lingo of today's youth. It is slowly working its way into our language, and today commercials include text lingo, newspapers, emails, and more. It isn't bad, but it isn't standard written English either. There is a place for both.

URL: This stands for Uniform Resource Locater, or a pointer that takes you to a specific domain name, or location, on the Web.

USB: The little rectangular ports, or holes, in the sides of gadgets and computers are usually there to connect

Universal Serial Bus additions, such as an i-POD, a Flash Drive, etc.

VBasic: This stands for Visual Basic, a programming code.

Virtual: In the beginning, this referred to something that wasn't real. Today, the virtual world is very real...it is just represented in an online format.

VLOG: Video Weblogs, shortened to VLOGs, is just a video version of an online diary or journal. With most laptops including webcams today, these are becoming more and more prevalent.

Web 2.0: The second generation of the World Wide Web which allows everyone, without any special equipment, software or expertise, to upload information and create user-created content in the online world. Also called "cloud computing."

Website: A single place that exists on the Web, made up of files and programming code. It has it's own domain in cyberspace.

World Wide Web: These are the files and software and programs that exist on all those computers that make up the Internet.

Made in the USA
Charleston, SC
10 May 2011